Infinite Playlists

Infinite Playlists

How to Have Conversations
[Not Conflict] with Your Kids
About Music

Todd Stocker

[with notes by
Nathan Stocker]

Kregel
Publications

Infinite Playlists: How to Have Conversations [Not Conflict] with Your Kids About Music

© 2010 by Todd Stocker

This is a revised and expanded edition, originally self-published by the author as *An 8-Track Parent in an MP3 World*.

Published by Kregel Publications, a division of Kregel, Inc., P.O. Box 2607, Grand Rapids, MI, 49501.

Library of Congress Cataloging-in-Publication Data
Stocker, Todd
Infinite playlists : how to have conversations (not conflict) with your kids about music / Todd Stocker ; with notes by Nathan Stocker.
  p.   cm.
Includes bibliographical references.
1. Music appreciation. 2. Music—Instruction and study—Parent participation. I. Stocker, Nathan. II. Title.
MT90.S76   2010   261.5'78—dc22   2010016275

ISBN 978-0-8254-3656-7

Printed in the United States of America

10 11 12 13 14/5 4 3 2 1

To my wife, Kellie.
We are walking the journey together.
I wouldn't have it any other way.

Infinite Playlists

contents

· ·

acknowledgments

. . . .

SPECIAL THANKS GO TO . . .

. . . my wife, Kellie, who makes everything I do even more meaningful.

. . . my son, Nathan, who kept giving me the eyes of youth during this writing project.

. . . my daughters, Makenzie and Madeline (one in heaven; one on earth), whose soaring voices inspire me to greater things.

. . . my parents, for instilling the gift of music in our family.

"I Love Rock 'n' Roll"

OK, I'LL ADMIT IT. I love 1980s Rock 'n' Roll. Not the fluffy, pre hip-hop, pop stuff, but the heavy distortions, consuming bass, and low driving drums that cause your heart to change rhythm. Give me Boston, BTO, Aerosmith, and the Scorpions and I'll be pounding out the beats to "Hurricane" on the steering wheel of my car. They just don't write 'em like that anymore!

This genre of music had always intrigued me. However, the reawakening of my Christian faith after college caused a dilemma. How could I listen to music and groups that were not considered "Christian" by the mainstream church?

Like many of you, I had stuffed my admission of the love of all types of music; I threw away many of my favorite college animal house classics and replaced them with Michael W. Smith, Newsboys, and Rich Mullins. I was a "new creation." I did not want to be reminded of my life as the "old creation." For me, the modern, secular artists and songs that I loved did not even get a listen once the Spirit set my faith on fire!

When Christian music became an official genre in the 1980s, there was an obvious difference in lyric and feel from songs topping the Top 40 charts. Scripture verses replaced seductive poetry, and major chords and folk percussion replaced minor chords and screaming guitars. Keyboard: good. Electric guitar: bad. And that is how I thought.

Secretly, however, when no one was around, I would sneak a dose of Van Halen's "Eruption" like a junkie taking a hit of hash behind the garage of his father's house. I felt dirty and somewhat evil. But the cool melodic guitar solo of Pink Floyd's "Comfortably Numb" stroked my musical heartstrings and I couldn't get enough. *How could this music be bad?* I thought.

Fast-forward to today. As of this book writing, I have a thirteen-year-old son who also loves music in its many forms. He is a better natural musician than I will ever be. He hears a drumbeat or guitar solo and can imitate it move by move, almost without error. (Honestly, it makes me sick and proud all at once!) He is a passionate music lover.

Accompanying my son's passion is a natural curiosity that most musicians possess. Let me explain. As musicians, we love music—all music. True, there may be styles and influences that we favor over and above others, but if we are honest, we love to sift through the sand of notes and beats to discover the jewels that make any genre glisten.

My son is no different. He loves discovering new (and old) guitar solos and fills. He loves to pound out the simple beats of The Cars and the more complicated drum fills from David Crowder. He has also discovered the joy of downloading music and now has the world of music at his clicker-tips!

With his insatiable appetite for music, I knew that eventually his taste and exposure to non-Christian music would prompt *the question*. What is *the question?* It came violently at me from him over the phone when he was twelve. He was on a vacation with my parents in San Francisco when they happened to venture into the Virgin Records store located on Stockton Street. This megastore houses thousands and thousands of music choices. When I picked up the phone, I could hear the thumping of Gwen Stefani in the background.

"Dad?" Nathan said.

"Yeah, Nate. What's up? Where are you?" I asked.

"Grandma and I are in the music store and I have to ask you a question."

I knew he wanted to buy a CD. I was expecting him to ask me my preference between Audio Adrenaline and Relient K (two very cool Christian bands) so I said, "Let me guess; you want to know if you can get a CD."

"Yes!" he said. "Which is better? Van Halen or Def Leppard?"

I'm convinced that electric buzzing sound I heard was my brain short-circuiting. *Van Halen or Def Leppard? How could I have raised such a rebel? Where did I go wrong? This must have been his mother's fault!* The words reverberated in my head.

In that moment, I knew that Nathan and I had to have a talk about music choice. I realized I needed to come to grips with my response as a parent to the desires and interest my son had for certain kinds of music. Hence this book.

Because music is such a touchy subject to many people both inside and outside the church, I want to be clear as to the purpose of this book. Let me start from the negative. The purpose of this book is not to convince you or your child to hate and reject "secular" music. Conversely, this writing is not to convince you or your child that only "Christian" music is the way to go. My goal in writing this book is threefold:

+ First, it is to provide you, the parent, with some under-standing of God's purpose for music.

+ Second, it is to offer guidelines that will help you and your child decide which music is acceptable and healthy and which is not.

+ Third and ultimately, my goal is to help foster healthy conversations between you and your child—conversations about music, honoring God, and the importance of correct decisions when it comes to music and media.

Nathan and I have worked through (and will continue to work through) an agreement that we believe honors God and allows one the freedom to choose music based on a framework that is both biblical and respectful. The principles and guidelines shared in this book work for us. They may or may not work for you, but again, having open conversations with your child is the goal, not an imposing set of rules.

One last caveat: Unless specified, I am not promoting specific artists, bands, songs, or genres of music. Most of the examples are just that—examples.

track 1

"Don't You Forget About Me"

Music: A Gift from God

I will sing a new song to you, O God;
on the ten-stringed lyre I will make music to you.
—PSALM 144:9

I have no use for cranks who despise music, because
it is a gift of God. . . . Next after theology, I give to
music the highest place and the greatest honor.
—MARTIN LUTHER

I CAN REMEMBER IT LIKE it was yesterday. I was in third grade; a snot-nosed, porky kid who loved pizza and hated the fact that popularity eluded me. Though I tried to cover up my uncoolness with bad jokes and a worse circle of friends, my status as outsider could not be shaken. I remember asking God why He did not make me popular. Why could other boys, on whom the girls and teachers focused, shoot baskets and run fast, but I could do neither? In misery, I would retreat to the comforting sounds of my John Thompson piano-lesson books and pound out "Edelweiss" from *Teaching Little Fingers That Play*. (Yes, I earned all of the gold stars for achievement.)

After trudging through that year, it became evident to me that while I would never be able to keep up with the football stars of my class, I played music . . . and I loved it. While other families were raking leaves or playing football on a Sunday afternoon, my family gathered in the living room around the piano singing everything from bluegrass to 1940s hits. My mother's fingers danced on the piano keys as my dad hammered out chords on the banjo. I usually strummed the guitar or standup bass while my brother and sisters sang out the verses of "Ma, He's Makin' Eyes at Me!" (If you know that song, you're older than I thought.)

My parents used this family time to practice for their side job, which was to provide nightly entertainment at a pizza joint called Shakey's Pizza Parlor. On occasion, and as a gimmick for tips, they would prop me up on a stool as I played the only three-chord banjo song I knew, "Little Brown Jug." The gimmick worked and we would come home with more grocery money and pizza than we could imagine!

After one such occasion, I went to school the next morning and noticed that something had changed. I was no longer the unknown, chubby kid. The most popular circles in the school talked with me and invited me to eat at their lunch table, the ultimate statement of popularity! Come to find out, the evening before, the most popular kid on campus ate at Shakey's and heard me plunk out my three-chord tune. He thought it was the coolest thing a third grader could do and told all of his friends. I was in. I was popular and the other kids truly appreciated that I had this gift called *music*.

I do not share this story to say that being a musician will make you popular. That is like saying being a politician will make you president or being a chef will make you Emeril Lagasse.

To me, that was my first realization that music was not just another created thing that God wove into the fabric of my being. In that moment, when someone else recognized the music in me, I knew that this was given to me *extrinsically*— from outside of myself.

Today I still hold this gift with trembling hands. I realize that the music I play is not mine but God's. I realize that the best use of this music is to give it back to Him as an offering and not to use it as a self-aggrandizing badge. Music is mysterious and at the same time obvious. It is simple yet complex. Each time I play it or sing it or hear it or dissect it, music teaches me something new—something new about life, about myself, about God, about others, about relationships, and about the world; music is a teacher.

Smokey Robinson is, perhaps, the most renowned entertainer in the music business. For more than forty-five years he has written and/or performed four thousand songs including "Tears of a Clown," "Just to See Her," and "Shop Around." Without hesitation, Robinson readily acknowledges God as a key part of his life. "I'm not a religious man," he says, "but I have a great relationship with God."

With the ups and downs of the music industry, Robinson quickly came to understand that there is a deeper, spiritual part of the human experience. "Do you think you're just flesh and blood, and that's it?" he asks. "I feel that . . . all the music I've ever done is a gift from God."[1]

. . . .

A gift is something given
voluntarily without payment coming
back to the giver.

. . . .

A gift is something given voluntarily without payment coming back to the giver. It is a sign of favor toward that person. It is an extension of love to the receiver. A true gift is completely free, no strings attached, no conditions or reservations. This is the type of gift God gives us through music.

God Himself values music as an expression of favor. Zephaniah 3:17 declares, "The LORD your God is with you, he is mighty to save. He will take great delight in you, he will quiet you with his love, he will rejoice over you with singing."

That verse hit me like a sound wave from heaven. God Himself sings! Picture that. God sitting down at the piano, the tips of His fingers gently rest on the keys as He contemplates His love for you. As those thoughts of you scroll through His mind, a gentle smile etches His face. He cannot contain Himself any longer. He cannot hold back that which has welled up inside. The expression of His favor for you erupts from His vocal chords as He lets the air of heaven flow from His lungs in a joyous chorus of melody over . . . you. He sings over you and me with rejoicing!

When I was a little boy, cowering under my parents' covers during a thunderstorm, Mom would calm me with, "It's OK, thunder is just God's voice singing a duet with the lightning." I always thought, *Why does He have to sing so loud!*

If God uses the gift of music personally, we better take a serious look at how we receive it, how we use it, and how we enjoy it.

Why God Gave Us Music

God gave music to the world for many reasons.

First, God gave us the gift of music as one of the vehicles through which we praise Him. Music is a response to what God has done for His people. It helps us respond to God's goodness and glory in a way unlike anything else. When God brought the children of Israel back from captivity, they worshipped Him, making music to His Name. Isaiah 51:11, says, "The ransomed [people] of the LORD will return. They will enter Zion with singing."

Take a quick journey through the psalms and you will see the constant call to praise the Lord with music all along the way:

> Praise the LORD with the harp; make music to him on the ten-stringed lyre. (Psalm 33:2)

It is good to praise the Lord and make music to your name, O Most High. (Psalm 92:1)

Let them praise his name with dancing and make music to him with tambourine and harp. (Psalm 149:3)

Whoa! Did you catch that last one? "Let them praise his name with *dancing.*" The d-word! I list that verse not for the sake of controversy but for another example that the arts, in all their *forms*, have been given to us as a gift to worship Him. Certain *expressions* of each form—whether music, dance, or PowerPoint backgrounds—should be used with careful discernment, because we want to offer our best to Him.[2] However, I digress.

. . . .
> Music is for our enjoyment, both
> personally and communally.
. . . .

Second, music is for our enjoyment, both personally and communally. Have you ever had one of those days? You know the ones I'm talking about. The "sleep through alarm, skip breakfast, late to work, forget the executive meeting, secretary quits, computer crashes, kids in the principal's office, collection agent calling, burn dinner, argument with the spouse, kids yelling, can't wait to go to bed" days? We've all had them. I can smell them coming when I look at my overstuffed date book. Call it therapy, call it crazy, but on those days, the amount of music I listen to increases exponentially! On days like that, light jazz fills my office. On days like that, praise and worship music fills my car. Music calms my inner beast and soothes my soul. God has given me the gift as a companion to enjoy and to share with others. Johann Sebastian Bach once said that music is "an agreeable harmony for the honor of God and the permissible delights of the soul."[3]

Not only is music an agreeable harmony for oneself and with God, but it is also a way of bringing people together. In the New Testament, the apostle Paul focused on the Christ-follower's life and gave specific instructions that help us maintain healthy relationships. Among the instructions is how we are to live and worship together in Christian community. In his letter to the Ephesians, Paul writes,

> Speak to one another with psalms, hymns and spiritual songs. Sing and make music in your heart to the Lord, always giving thanks to God the Father for everything, in the name of our Lord Jesus Christ. (Ephesians 5:19–20)

Our response to God's goodness and the connection that we have with other believers is the joining of our voices together and the making of music to Him; beautiful, joyful music that praises Him for what He's done and who He is. We celebrate together through music that He is the only God of the universe and that He is the Creator of it all. Everything! Things physical and things spiritual. Rocks, trees, spirits, air, music; it all flows from the hand of the Almighty.

> Every good and perfect gift is from above, coming down from the Father of the heavenly lights, who

does not change like shifting shadows. (James 1:17)

Unfortunately, many who
call themselves Christians do
not see the world this way.
They see labels, they see stig-
mas, and they see unredeem-
able black-and-white lines. As
a result, they miss out on so
much beauty in life and suc-
cumb to a belief that this life
is just the waiting room for
heaven.

> **Nathan's Note**
> Music is something that I can't
> understand. I don't know why
> it soothes my soul and the truth
> is, I don't care why or how.
> I only know that it does and
> that's enough for me. When I'm
> totally bored, happy, or angry,
> I play music. Music helps me
> to express and/or release my
> emotions. Who wouldn't want
> something like that in their life?
> I mean, come on!

Have you ever been in a waiting room? Uncomfortable
chairs, unadorned walls, a receptionist locked behind a glass
cage, a few fake and dusty plants, and cheesy elevator music
leaking out of the sagging, used-to-be-white paneled ceiling.
Yuck! These are the people that give true Christ-followers a
bad name. These are the people who look like they've been
weaned on a dill pickle.

Play the black-and-white label too far and you'll end up like
the monks in the Middle Ages that completely removed themselves from society in fear that they might become tainted
with "the world." Cue evil music.

God never intended for Christians to live cloistered. This
world is beautiful, a masterpiece painted by the Master Artist
Himself. Every blade of grass, every flutter of a baby's eyelash,
every melody from the heart of an artist gives testimony to
God's creative greatness. The issue we need some discernment

about, especially in the music world, is the misuse and abuse of what God intends for good.

Author and speaker Louie Giglio wrote,

> I think that all music—not just Christian music but all music—is worship music, because every song is amplifying the value of something. . . . There's a trail of our time, our affections, our allegiance, our devotion, our money. That trail leads to a throne, and whatever's on that throne is what we worship. We're all doing a great job of it because God has created us to be worshipers. The problem is that a lot of us have really bad gods.[4]

Understanding the dynamics of the spiritual battle behind music is instrumental in keeping both parent and child safe from the Devil's harmful influences.

The Devil at Work

The Devil's primary objectives are to defame God, to oppose Him at every turn, and to destroy God's work in the world and in people. The Devil will, by any means possible, do everything in his power to accomplish his goals. The Bible describes him as a predator on the hunt for prey:

> Be self-controlled and alert. Your enemy the devil prowls around like a roaring lion looking for someone to devour. (1 Peter 5:8)

While he is powerful, he is not original. He does not have

the ability to create anything new. Only God can do that. The Devil's tactic is to take what God has given as a gift and distort it for his own purposes.

Take, for example, the distortion of the gift of sexual intercourse. Sex is a gift that God created for people's enjoyment, to populate the earth, and to give Him glory. It is only to be experienced within the context of a marriage relationship. Satan uses this great gift, distorts its purpose and meaning, and causes many to stumble and fall, destroying families and individuals. Thousands of pornography Web sites are available to anyone with Internet access and a desire for getting a sexual fix. Countless opportunities for "casual sex" are available on many school campuses and every darkened street corner.

Unfortunately, our society now sees this misuse of sex as normal, and the created life that results from that union is considered expendable. What God intends for good, Satan distorts. What God gives as a gift, Satan tries to destroy.

. . . .

What God intends for good, Satan distorts. What God gives as a gift, Satan tries to destroy.

. . . .

The Devil has many titles in the Bible but the one that seldom gets a spotlight is noted in Paul's letter to the Ephesians:

As for you, you were dead in your transgressions and sins, in which you used to live when you followed the ways of this world and of the ruler of the kingdom of the air, the spirit who is now at work in those who are disobedient. (Ephesians 2:1–2)

Satan is called "the ruler of the kingdom of the air." Many theologians suggest that the air talked about here refers to the means through which communication happens. Speaking, singing, writing, texting—these are all forms of communication that the Devil twists and confuses to disrupt healthy relationships.

I remember writing an e-mail to a colleague asking a question about a song that was used in worship the week prior. A few minutes after I hit the send key, the person to whom I wrote the e-mail stormed into my office and demanded to know why I was accusing him of blasphemy. I was confused. I thought it was a cool song and wanted to use it for an upcoming event. He read into the e-mail something that was not intended.

I'm sure you've been speaking with someone and have completely missed the point of what they were saying. Maybe you were told by your spouse to pick up the kids from school but did not hear the words "at 3:15." By 3:30, your children were devastated that mommy and daddy had forgotten them. This mishap ripples through your relationship with your family. To your spouse, this simple misunderstanding actually looks like you intentionally dismissed a request.

The Devil rules the air. Anything that we hear from "the air" is in his crosshairs to disrupt. What we hear from the TV, movies, radio, music, Internet—communication of any sort—is used by him to create chaos in our relationships with others and ultimately with God. How many times have you had a conversation with your child and he or she interprets what you said differently from what you intended? If you are like me, this happens often. Many theologians believe that this misinterpretation is the work of Satan, trying to confuse the communication lines to create conflict.

True or not, one thing we know for sure: God's gift of music, with its heart pounding rhythms, sweet poetry, and flowing melody, is an easy target for Satan.

As parents, we need to be aware of Satan's power, but not threatened by it. God has already conquered Satan. His days of prowling are limited and he knows it. The beautiful aspect of God's grace is that we are under God's protection and He has given us His Holy Spirit to keep the work of Satan from taking hold in our personal lives and in our families. As it says in 1 John,

> You, dear children, are from God and have overcome them [evil spirits], because the one who is in you is greater than the one who is in the world. (1 John 4:4)

Recap

✔ Music is a gift that is given to us by God! He Himself takes to song when He thinks about His love for you and me.

✔ God gave us music as one of the many ways that we can praise Him. He also gave it for our pleasure.

✔ As with any gift that God gives, the Enemy twists it and makes it ugly.

track 2

"You've Got a Hold on Me"

The Effects of Music

I will sing to the LORD, for he is highly exalted.
The horse and its rider he has hurled into the sea.
—EXODUS 15:1

Where words fail, music speaks.
—HANS CHRISTIAN ANDERSEN

IN THE FILM *The Shawshank Redemption*, Ellis Boyd "Red" Redding (Morgan Freeman) tells the story of Andy Dufresne (Tim Robbins)—a young, successful banker wrongly convicted of murdering his wife in 1947 and sentenced to two consecutive life terms at Shawshank Prison.

At one point in the film, the guards give Dufresne the task of sorting through a whole load of classical records that were donated to the prison. While looking through the boxes, he finds and plays a beautiful operatic piece, even though it's against prison regulations. Aware of the rule infringement, Dufresne chooses to lock himself in the sound booth and switches on the PA system that reaches the whole prison—the cells, the yard, and the hospital. He plays the music full blast through the speakers. Everyone in the whole prison stops what they are doing and listens. At this point Morgan Freeman's character comments:

> I have no idea to this day what those two Italian ladies were singing about. Truth is, I don't want to know. Some things are best left unsaid. I'd like to think they were singing about something so beautiful it can't be expressed in words. It makes your heart ache because of it. I tell you those voices soared. Higher and farther than anyone in the great place dared to dream. It was like some beautiful bird flapped into our drab little cage and made those walls dissolve away. And for the briefest of moments, every last man in Shawshank felt free.[1]

Nathan's Note

The mood of music is extremely important. Let's say that all you listen to is dark, "emo" musical bands. What do you think the effect on your attitude will be? More than likely you'd want to wear dark clothes, dye your hair, escape from everyone around you, and live by yourself in darkness with the haunting old spirits of Christmas past. OK, maybe not that last part, but your attitude will change.

Music has the power to help us forget our present circumstances and transport us to another place in time. It can move us. It can mold us. Music is power.

The word "power" means "a strength or force exerted or capable of being exerted."[2] When the waves of the ocean slam against the shore and cause the ground to shake, that's power! When a steady drip wears away granite, that's power! When the engine of an F16 fighter jet flies low over a house, causing its windows to rattle in their frames, or when someone you love whispers in your ear, "I love you," that's power! Large or small, any force that moves people deeply is powerful.

Many studies have shown that music can affect change. It changes the listener's mood, focus, and even plan of action. That change can be positive or negative.

One such study found that teenagers between the ages of twelve and seventeen who listen to music that contains degrading sexual lyrics were more likely to participate in sexual activity than others whose music lyrics simply talked about love and romance:

Between 2002 and 2004, the researchers carried out follow-up interviews to track the sexual developments in the teens' lives. Around 51 percent of teens whose music collection consisted mainly of sexually degrading music began having sex within two years of the three-year study as against 29 percent of those who did not enjoy such music.[3]

Their conclusion? "Reducing the amount of degrading sexual content in popular music or reducing young people's exposure to music with this type of content could help delay the onset of sexual behavior." They also state, "A recent analysis of the content of television shows, movies, magazines, newspapers, and music popular among teens demonstrated that sexual content is much more prevalent in popular music lyrics than in any other medium."[4]

"A lot of teens think that's the way they're supposed to be," says seventeen-year-old Natasha Ramsey. She is editor of SEXETC.COM, a Rutgers University Web site on teenage sexual health. "They think that's the cool thing to do." She agrees that music is a major decision driver. "Teens will try to deny it; they'll say: 'No, it's not the music.' But it IS the music! That has one of the biggest impacts on our lives."[5]

. . . .

Music encompasses all parts of our humanity: our emotions, our physical bodies, and our spiritual health.

. . . .

Music affects us in ways we often don't even realize. For instance, our bodies operate in rhythms—the beat of our hearts, the blinking of our eyes, the breathing of our lungs. The beat of music can increase or decrease our breathing, heart rate, and other physical functions of our bodies. Music can also dive deep into our souls. Little else can change our attitudes, our feelings, and our thoughts as quickly and as thoroughly as music. Music encompasses all parts of our humanity: our emotional state, our physical bodies, and our spiritual health. As we will see later, it is important to understand the impact of music in all three of these areas when choosing music.

The Emotional Impact

Emotions are more than feelings. They are rhythms in the symphony of our lives. The Reverend Basil Nortz, theologian and priest, writes,

> There are certain natural bodily motions which commonly accompany man's feelings of joy, anger, hope, sorrow, fear, despair, love, hate and courage. Music is capable of imitating these same movements, and so evoke these feelings in the soul. In this way, music is a natural and universal language, which is not learned, but immediately and connaturally felt. It is true that we can learn to associate certain memories and feelings with certain kinds of music due to repeated experiences. Nevertheless, for the most part, music, by its very melody, harmony, rhythm, etc., expresses specific emotions. There is no need to teach a child "this is happy music," or "this is sad music." As soon as happy music is played the child begins to dance. Whereas, when sad music is played a different reaction occurs.[6]

When I was finishing college, I felt uncertain about my future. What was I going to do for a job? Would I ever find a woman who would put up with me forever? Were my parents going to start charging me rent? (OK, I was a little sheltered.) For a twenty-year-old, these are serious questions that can have long-lasting impact.

During that disconcerting time, I would often express my frustration and confusion through music. When depressed, I would hammer out a Pink Floyd tune on the piano. When feeling a bit more upbeat, a tight chord progression from Boston or Petra would sing out from my guitar strings. Music calms my weary soul.

In 1 Samuel 16, King Saul was feeling the consequences of putting his pride above God's commands. He disobeyed God and felt the impact of his sin. The Bible says that God had even allowed a spirit to torment him. Saul was having a major attack of depression! In the midst of this stressful and heart wrenching time, Saul told his servants to bring David to play for him.

> David would take his harp and play. Then relief would come to Saul; he would feel better, and the evil spirit would leave him. (1 Samuel 16:23)

Music is so powerful that even evil spirits flee from it! God has designed music to be a spokesperson for our emotions. Phrasing, melody, rhythm, and beat all contribute to the emotional impact of a song. Beyond influencing our emotions, music can be a tool through which we express our emotions. Musician Lenny Kravitz once said, "Music is my life. It is a reflection of what I go through."[7] I completely agree.

. . . .

    Music is my life. It is a reflection
         of what I go through.
              -Lenny Kravitz

. . . .

The Physical Impact

At the beginning of every year, I join the masses in making the resolution to get back in shape. I usually buy new running shoes, new workout shirts, and a new water bottle. I also find my MP3 player and load it with the latest songs. Why is this such a vital piece of my attire? Is it because I want to look cool when I run? No. Is it because I want to tune out the sound of other people's gasps and wheezings as they pass me on the track? Not really. It is because the music that seeps from the earbuds and fills my mind motivates me to run faster and farther. My stride naturally matches the rhythm of the music that spurs me on.

Researchers believe that music gets to us because we are rhythmic beings, with rhythm in respiration, heartbeats, brain waves, gait, muscles, and speech. The impact of music appears to be in the way musical sounds reach and affect the brain.

An article in *Vibrant Life* examines the relationship between the waves of music and the pulses of the brain:

> In 1896, an Italian physician, caring for a 13-year-old boy who had a healed skull wound through which brain pulsations could be observed, experimented with music. He reported that it did indeed affect the pulsations, or rhythms of the brain. He noted that

high notes seemed to produce bigger changes than those of lower pitch.[8]

Musicologist Julius Portnoy found that not only can music "change metabolism, affect muscular energy, raise or lower blood pressure, and influence digestion," but also "It may be able to do all these things more successfully . . . than any other stimulants that produce those changes in our bodies."[9]

An article posted on Incrediblehorizons.com says,

There are at least three neuro-physical healing processes triggered by music:

1. Music is nonverbal so it can move through the brain's auditory cortex directly to the center of the limbic system. This system governs emotional experiences and basic metabolic responses such as body temperature, blood pressure, and heart rate. It can help create new neuro-pathways in the brain, as well.

2. Music can activate the flow of stored memory and imagined material across the corpus callosum (the bridge between the left and right hemispheres of the brain) helping the two work in harmony. This stimulates the immune system.

3. Music can excite peptides in the brain and stimulate the production of endorphins, which are natural opiates secreted by the hypothalamus, which produces a feeling of natural euphoria, shifting mood and emotion.[10]

Simply put, our bodies react to the rhythms that surround it. Walk by a restaurant in New Orleans that has an in-house jazz trio and unconsciously, your steps begin to echo the "boom-chick-boom-chick" of the drums. Turn on the radio while you're driving and your fingers and hands begin to tap to the rhythm on the steering wheel. Because we are rhythmic creations, every note and beat can affect how our body responds physically.

The Spiritual Impact

The previous chapter described how music is a gift received and a gift given. In essence, the spiritual impact of music is present in the exchanging of the music gift, first from God to us and then back from us to God.

However, there are two aspects of music that could be classified as "spiritual." There are many different definitions of what it means when something is classified as "spiritual." It could mean having the nature of a spiritual being. It could mean something that cannot be touched or perceived. It could even mean something that dwells in another dimension.

While all of these are true, music can be deemed "spiritual" first, because of its use by the Holy Spirit to connect a person to a basic perception of God. In the King James Version of Psalm 22:3, the psalmist says, "But thou art holy, O thou that inhabitest the praises of Israel." (I love that old English.) Simply put, God can be found when we praise Him! This is not saying that music saves a person. Only a Spirit-given faith in Jesus Christ can do that. But God promises to be present when praise—in our context, *music*—is heard, sung, and played. The first spiritual aspect of lyric and tone recognizes the presence of God in the presence of music.

The second spiritual aspect comes from the power of a song to transport you to another time and place. If you have ever heard a song and remembered a situation tied to that song, you understand the spiritual impact of music. A lyric or melody can transport us to another place in time; hearing a certain rhythm can cause us to relive a chapter in our lives. From that standpoint, music has a spiritual impact.

Several years ago, my father took a group of his music students, of which I was one, on a choir tour of the former Soviet Union. We were privileged to sing in some of the greatest churches and concert halls in their nation. With the fall of communism, many of these venues were just starting to allow foreign singing groups to perform.

One of those places was the Estonia Concert Hall in Tallinn, Estonia. This beautiful, acoustically perfect space required no present-day technology to amplify sound. Every note we sang blossomed like a new flower in the morning of a spring day. The music filled the room and wrapped us all in its inescapable embrace. It was of heaven!

Even though we had permission to give this concert, there were strict instructions from the government that we could not sing the words to Estonia's national anthem. Communism had lost the battle but it still had a grip on the society.

Our performance was stellar—no surprise there. However, the most powerful moment came at the very end of the concert. As the final notes of our last, *program printed* number rang out, our seventy-five-member choir, in single file, came down off the stage stairs on each side of the platform and encircled the audience.

Sitting three feet away from me was an elderly couple that

must have been in their eighties; he in his military uniform from forty years ago (this is typical of veterans in that society) and she in her babushka and clogs. Next to them sat, I presumed, their grandchild, a kid roughly the age of fourteen. As we took our places around the audience, I sensed an odd tension between them and us. The elderly man, with a furrowed brow, cast a skeptical look at me. Then, my father blew a single note on a pitch pipe, which echoed off the walls. We began humming. No words, no loud symphony, just the sweet melody of—yes, you guessed it—Estonia's national anthem.

I was not prepared for what happened next. Most of the crowd started weeping. Not just a trickle of tears, but a full out river. They had not heard their national anthem presented publicly in more than sixty years! Moved by the music and the patriotism for which it called, many elderly people slowly rose to their feet including that couple closest to me. I noticed the elderly man grabbing the upper arm of the slouching teen and pulling him up.

There we all stood. Transported back to a time when life was free. When people lived in peace and prosperity. The fears of the last sixty years melted away in that moment. The music from our choir had transported those few hundred people back in time, and we loved it. The societal walls and divisions that we carried were gone. Our two countries, that were thousands of miles apart physically and even more so politically, were woven together by history, by intimacy . . . by music.

The last sounds of that song faded and there was a deafening silence. Then, the whole place went crazy. Applause, hugs, kisses on the cheeks, more hugs, more kisses, some *bravos* echoing from the crowd and the gracious love of the people overwhelmed us. Then the formerly stern man ran over (yes, *ran*), grabbed me, and squeezed. Not the kind of gentle caress a mother gives her child but a full-on, grandfatherly bear-hug squeeze that made my cheeks turn red and my eyes bulge! I was so caught up in the moment I did not immediately realize he had picked me up and was spinning me around like a father does with his three-year-old son in the backyard. I didn't care.

Even as I write these words, my eyes are tearing up. The musty smell of the man's old uniform is filling my nose and I am, at this moment, once again in Estonia.

Recap

✔ Music is a powerful force. There's no doubt about that. It can change emotions, actions, attitudes, and decisions.

✔ Music affects us in three ways:

1. Emotionally: Soothing melodies and sounds can calm us; hard, rocking beats can get us fired up.

2. Physically: Music gets to us because we are rhythmic beings, with rhythm in respiration, heartbeats, brain waves, gait, and speech.

3. Spiritually: Hearing a certain melody or rhythm can take us to another time and place in our spirits.

track 3

"I'm a Little Bit Country . . .
I'm a Little Bit Rock 'n' Roll"

Understanding Music Genre

*Speak to one another with psalms,
hymns and spiritual songs. Sing and make music
in your heart to the Lord.*

—Ephesians 5:19

*Well, we play Country music;
we're just not sure what country it is.*

—Jerry Jeff Walker

Every morning the battle ensues. "I want this station!" "No! I want to listen to that station!" Since each of my three children has a different taste in music, they fight vehemently for the radio tuner! Eventually, I step in and exercise what I have deemed *driver privilege*—the driver gets to choose what type of music we listen to during our commute. In other words, I get to choose the *genre* of music. Usually it is inspirational Christian rock (we have an awesome station here in Houston). Sometimes we actually turn the radio off and just talk! What a concept.

Genre Defined

Dictonary.com defines the word *genre* as "a class or category of artistic endeavor having a particular form, content, technique, or the like."[1] In other words, the elements of the genre logically fit together.

Picture a room in your house; say, the bathroom. Your bathroom has a certain feel, look, and functionality that none of the other rooms in your house possess. Now let's say your family wanted to watch a movie together and someone had the bright idea of watching it in the bathroom. As strange as it may sound, a spark of creativity challenged your family to act on the idea. Now, to watch the movie you would have to haul in the TV/DVD equipment, cram in chairs, and so on. Since a bathroom's design and purpose is not intended for family movie night, the idea would probably be thrown out the window. Couches do not fit in the "genre" of a bathroom. Just like a bathtub does not fit the "genre" of a garage.

Translate that illustration into the music realm. A music genre is that *room* of music with a certain style, beat, mood, flavor, tempo, and purpose. If you enter the soft Jazz *room*, your heartbeat will slow and you'll feel like sipping an espresso. If you enter the metal rock *room*, you'll sense a dramatic increase in your blood pressure and will expect to be attacked by the shredding of the guitars.

I like almost every genre of music—Rock 'n' Roll, Contemporary Christian, Jazz, Rap, and Reggae. Just like walking through the rooms in my house, I enjoy the different genres of music based on my circumstances of the moment. Like our earlier discussion on the emotions of music, I tend to listen to music that speaks to the emotion of my day. Often, I'll set my MP3 player to shuffle and listen to U2 Pop/Rock back-to-back with New Age pianist Lorie Line.

One of the most important aspects of genre that you need to understand is this: Genre has more to do with the *feel* of a song than with the *words* of a song. You and I have heard classic songs reset into a different feel. A friend of mine recently sent me a CD entitled *Lounge Worship*. The disc was a collection of great praise songs that were arranged and recorded in the Jazz genre . . . I love it!

Christian and *Secular* Music— Is there a difference?

Reread the title of this section. Notice the use of a small word that has huge ramifications for our whole subject matter. Yup, you caught it. The use of the word *and*. There is intentionality in the use of that word. Suppose this section title was "Christian *versus* Secular Music." It sounds like a title ring fight, a brawl of cosmic proportions between good and evil. And as Christians, we are the ones stuck in the middle, being forced to choose music from one side or the other. I have always struggled with this sharp distinction.

Truthfully, there is a spiritual battle that rages even though in Christ we're already declared victorious. However, we need to be sensitive to the hard categories of "Christian" and "Secular." A car dealership with a Christian fish in its logo does not necessarily operate with Christian principles. Just because a bookstore sells New Age books doesn't mean it doesn't have Bibles.

Yes, the categories of Christian and Secular music are helpful to an extent, but too often we, as well-meaning parents, throw the baby out with the bathwater. We label something *secular* as if it were the spawn of Satan.

What is it that makes a song "Christian"? What is it that tags a song as "Secular"? Is it the artist? Is it the record label? What is it? The answer is *the lyrics*. (Stop and think about that last sentence.)

I heard Rick Warren, pastor of Saddleback Church in California, say that there is no such thing as Christian music, only Christian lyrics.

> **Nathan's Note**
> Sometimes I hear five seconds of some songs and I judge that they are secular just from the beginning. Then I listen to the words and I'm like, "Cool, they're talking about God." Don't judge a song until you hear the lyrics. I love the Jonas Brothers' music (no, I don't think they're cute). That band is labeled as a "secular" band, yet they're from a Christian family, but I hear bands that sing about the same stuff and they are labeled "Christian." That confuses me. I wonder what would happen if the Brothers put *Jesus, Lord,* or *Savior* in one of their songs.

Mostly, that is true. The lyrics are the messenger of the song. However, the rhythms are not neutral. Consistent hard-driving beats have a physical, spiritual, and emotional effect on the listener. (This understanding will be important when we talk about the guidelines for choosing music.) There are cultures that use strong beats in demonic rituals to usher the participant into a trancelike state. They can lull a person into a world of illusion and fantasy that, when taken too far, can cause a breakdown in the listener's perception of reality.[2]

Lyrics are the words to the song. Lyrics tell the story and carry the message. The words of Christian music usually describe life with God, life with others, and struggles that all of us encounter. For example, Christian artist Brandon Heath wrote the song, "I'm Not Who I Was" describing how different he became because of his encounter with Grace. He is writing it to someone who knew him before that and conveys his desire that this person be able to see the great change in his life. Powerful stuff.

Secular music can have the same kind of power. The country rock band Rascal Flatts performs a song called "Bless the Broken Road." The lyrics speak of a person's thankfulness to God for the road of struggle that ultimately leads him to the one he loves. How beautiful is that!

What we must remember is that God is not in one thing and not in the other. He is everywhere at all times, creating, deleting, renewing everything around us. There is nothing that has been created that does not first come from Him. The Bible says that "without him nothing was made that has been made" (John 1:3).

That Was Then, This Is Now . . .

Along with being a pastor, I was also the worship leader in my church for several years. As a self-diagnosed sufferer of Attention Deficit Disorder, I was always looking to add a little something different or extra to the praise set that led people in worship. Some things worked, others didn't. I was always on the hunt for ideas and borrowed them from both inside and outside the church world.

One Sunday, the topic of the message centered simply on how much we love God and why. Well, I was tired of doing the standards and I was looking for something different. I was driving to an appointment that week thinking about the upcoming song list and turned on the local 80s rock station for inspiration. The song "Mony, Mony," recorded by Billy Idol, blared through the speakers. I cranked it!

There is a part of the song, toward the end, where Billy repeats the title over and over as the song builds toward the last chorus. (You're singing it in your head, aren't you?) The thought came to me to use that portion of the song as a break-out in the middle of the praise song "I Love Your Grace" by Rick Founds. Change the words to "I love you Lord Lo-Lo-Lord yeah I do" and it's a hit!

My heart was pounding with excitement as I went with the rewrite to my worship team.

"Now guys, you're going to love this!" I began. "Our congregation is expecting us to do this praise song the same way we've always done it. Verse, chorus, verse, chorus, chorus, 8-bar bass solo, chorus, end. But I think we should shake it up a bit. So check this out." And I launched into my work of art.

Jamming through the first verse and chorus, I had my team with me. Even in rehearsal, the Holy Spirit broke through our music. Then I got to the pièce de résistance . . . my masterwork of creativity.

I sang ". . . but You know I love Your presence most of all." Then I broke out into "I love You Lord Lo-Lo-Lord, yeah I do" and repeated it just as Billy Idol would've had he been a worship leader. When the last strings stopped vibrating on my guitar that is when I heard it—stunned silence deafening the room.

"Well? Isn't it powerful and cool?!" Again silence . . . until one of the team members spoke.

"It works verbally, but mentally, all I can think of is drinking ungodly amounts of alcohol at a party where I lost my virginity."

I threw away the score.

That experience reminds me of another facet of our discussion called context. Context is simply the situation in which the music is presented. The context of a song can make or break the music.

. . . .

> Context is simply the situation
> in which the music is presented.
> The context of a song can make
> or break the music.

. . . .

Have you ever noticed the different reactions of people to the same song? Mostly, people accept or reject a song based on personal taste. But often people relate the song to an experience when they first heard that song—a party, a wedding, a first dance, whatever. Or they may relate it to a period in their lives when the song took on a significant meaning for them—junior high, first girlfriend, the loss of a loved one. Context is very important.

The seminary I attended was beautiful. Set in the middle of St. Louis with tall trees and rolling hills, the gothic looking buildings could have come straight out of a small village in Germany. In the center of the campus is a tall bell tower that housed a carillon, an organlike instrument that has a stationary set of bells instead of pipes. When the musician plays a note on the keyboard, a corresponding bell rings out.

During the spring and summer, the seminary would host concerts. The musician would play Bach, Handel, and Mozart melodies and people would sit on the lawn with a blanket and listen to the beautiful sounds of the carillon bells filling the air.

On one occasion, we were sitting with a friend, talking and listening to the bells, when all of a sudden he stopped, looked up at the carillon and began chuckling. I asked him what was so funny.

"Do you hear the melody line?"

"Yes . . . so what?" I said.

"That's the Michigan State fight song!" he said. Apparently, the musician was bored with the same repertoire and decided to change it up a bit. Worked for me! The funny part of the experience was hearing the raving from the people on the lawn over the "classical melody that must have been written by Handel." If they only knew.

Recap

- ✔ *Genre* is defined as a class or category of artistic endeavor having a particular form, content, technique, or the like. In other words, the elements of the genre logically fit together.

- ✔ The music genre labels of "Christian" and "Secular" can be deceiving. There are songs on both sides of the aisle that can cross over.

- ✔ The lyrics, rhythm, and context of a song will play key roles in discussions with your child about music.

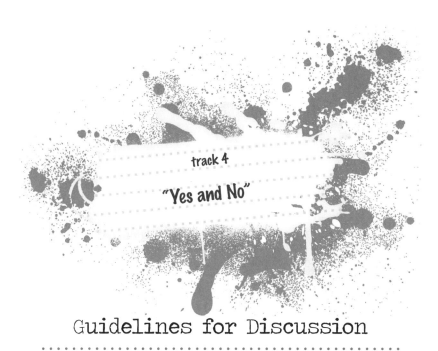

track 4

"Yes and No"

Guidelines for Discussion

You say, "I am allowed to do anything"—but not everything is good for you. You say, "I am allowed to do anything"—but not everything is beneficial.
—1 CORINTHIANS 10:23 NLT

Music is the friend who is always faithful, never condemning, and can change the direction of my day.
—ANONYMOUS

GROWING UP, WE LIVED across the street from a large neighborhood park. Every evening, all of the neighborhood kids would gather to play kick-the-can. The goal of the game was to kick the can before the person guarding it could catch you. If you did, everyone on your team who had been caught ran free. If you did not, you'd be caught and put in "jail."

After picking the guardian of the can, we would decide on the boundaries. If you ventured out of bounds, you were considered caught and had to go to jail. As long as you stayed in the boundaries, you had great freedom to run and hide and duck for cover. It was great fun!

> **Nathan's Note**
> When I want to get a song, I throw a ton of questions at my dad about it. I'm thirteen. I need to know *why* a song is good or not. Sometimes I don't like his final answer, but he's the dad and I should trust him. What he says goes. It's for the best.

The guidelines in which Nathan and I make our music decisions together are like those boundaries. They offer great freedom and safety within the agreed-upon bounds. By setting up the following "boundaries," Nathan and I know exactly what an acceptable song is and what it is not.

Together, we have come up with these guidelines. As stated in the introduction, the guidelines work for us and I hope they will help you and your child enter into a conversation about the music to which you both are listening.

The Working Guidelines

When Nathan asked me if he could buy a Def Leppard CD, I had to make a decision right there on the spot. Over the phone, two thousand miles apart, Nathan and I came up with the number one, most important guideline: The Parent makes the final decision, but not without input from the Child.

....

    The Parent makes the final decision,
    but not without input from the Child.

....

Like it or not, parents (or those who would be considered the head of the household) are responsible to God for the family under their care. This includes all aspects of health: physical, emotional, and spiritual. The Bible says that parents are one of the authorities under whom children are to live and grow (see Colossians 3:20).

God has placed great importance and responsibility on your parental position within the family. Therefore, it is not OK to allow your children to listen to lyrics that could poison their souls. Think of it this way: you would never allow your children to drink gasoline even if it was their choice to do so. Neither should you let your children *drink* music that could cripple them forever.

Along with this guideline, Moms and Dads, you need to make sure your child knows the reason behind the decision. If you want to build a wall between your child and you, simply make a decision and seal it with a "because I said so." Bad move. Your children are more apt to accept a decision if they know the "why" behind it. Isn't this true in your own life?

If you were to get a traffic ticket and you asked the officer "why," how likely would you be to accept the answer "because I said so"?

A series of commonsense questions will help weed out music that should be banned from your home, without the dreaded *because I said so*. These form the basic guidelines from which Nathan and I discuss the approval of songs, so that, together, we can say *because the guidelines say so*.

Question 1
What do the lyrics say?

The past few years have marked an increase in music that is downloaded over the Internet rather than purchased in a store. People carry around MP3 players and cell phones instead of bulky CD players. Parents may not even be fazed by their children's music choices because they no longer have to hear it as the music streams directly from player to earbuds. Without CD jackets laying around the house with the printed lyrics handily and condemningly available, parents may overlook the need to know what words are being spoken to their children.

Remember, along with the music itself, the lyrics carry the message of the song. The lyrics are often straightforward. They mean what they say and they say what they mean. Hawk Nelson's song "California" speaks plainly about the desire to find a better life in the golden state. Pretty simple.

Sometimes the lyrics say one thing and mean quite another—double entendre—the words have a double meaning. When I was growing up, the transformation of the word "gay" took place. In my parents' day, to be gay meant to be

happy, joyful, and lighthearted. By the time I entered middle
school, the word's meaning changed to describe someone who
practiced the homosexual lifestyle. There are certain words
and phrases that seem harmless to our "old" cultured ears but
have taken on a new, inappropriate meaning. Parents, you may
need to do some research into the slang of today's youth culture.[1] (Check out that endnote!)

. . . .

Appropriate lyrics are nonnegotiable.

. . . .

Appropriate lyrics are nonnegotiable. There are multiple
Web sites where they can be found. Do an Internet search on
the song title and type "lyrics" behind it and you have your list.
(If it's a common title, it may help to add the artist's name.)
Another great resource is Wikipedia.com. (While this is gen-
erally not a credible source for student research papers, it is a
good place on the net to research song lyrics.) Type in the title
of the song and it gives you its history, a bit about the band,
and sometimes what the composer of the song meant by the
lyrics.

However, I suggest that you have your child look up the lyrics first, print them out, and give them to you. For every song
that Nathan wants to download, he needs to provide me with
the lyrics. By having him look at the lyrics first, he is learning
to take responsibility for discerning what is good and avoiding
what is bad. This gives him a sense of confidence and ownership in the process. Nathan now eliminates songs even before
he asks me because he knows what is acceptable and what is
not.

We have even turned the whole process into a fun time of

song searching. The Web site from which we often download songs carries international as well as American tunes. There are bands we have never heard of before; genres that we dissect and analyze. However, we examine all of these within the boundaries upon which we agree.

Once we began reading the lyrics together, we decided that there were three "nails in the coffin" for a song—lyrical disqualifiers that keep it from our playlists.

First, the song is dropped if the lyrics denounce God in any way. Marilyn Manson's song "Dead God" is off the list. Not because of the title but because the lyrics make statements that attack God's character, the act of Grace through Jesus' death and resurrection, and the active part He plays in our lives. It is blatant blasphemy in the form of rock music. Sad, but this type of disregard for the Giver of musical talent is all over the place.

There is a gray area here. There are some lyrics that do not denounce God but speak some incorrect theology about God. In other words, some lyrics speak about the spiritual world in an incorrect way. The song "From a Distance" written by Julie Gold and sung by Bette Midler is a good example. It gives the hearer the impression that God is not involved in our everyday lives and is indifferent at best. However, God says that He is present in our every move, our every breath, and our every circumstance. Psalm 139:7–8 says,

> Where can I go from your Spirit?
> Where can I flee from your presence?
> If I go up to the heavens, you are there;
> If I make my bed in the depths, you are there.

Nathan's Note

One of my favorite songs is "Dead" by a band named My Chemical Romance. It's just got a ring to it that I love. Listening to the lyrics I think to myself, "hmm, nothing wrong with them." Then I get to the end of the song. Oh boy, there's the F-Bomb, and it ruins the entire song. What's up with that?? One word blows the entire masterpiece of musicianship to pieces. I hate it when bands do that! What's the point of using language like that? You don't have to ruin what you write with language like that. The cuss word may rhyme. The cuss word may flow with the song, but even if the shoe fits, it still might look ugly.

Another common phrase or teaching that comes up says, "Believe in yourself" or variations of that. Watch this one. Its roots are a mix of Eastern mysticism and New Age. Now I am all for self-confidence and praising God for the gifts and talents that He gives, but I also know that God is the only one in whom we can trust and believe. (That is a topic for a different book.)

When Nathan brings songs like this to me, we talk about its implications. I ask him what he thinks about the message of the lyrics and what he thinks is the truth. I use those songs as teachable moments and have accepted about half of them based on our conversation together. Again, acceptance of songs with ambiguous teaching needs to be based on truth and your discussion about the truth.

Secondly, we do not allow songs that use cuss words or take the name of God in vain. Even though my son goes to a Christian school, he is already exposed to some heavy-duty language. He already knows the words and phrases and hears them regularly at school. The music he listens to does not need to reinforce that language. In fact, those words implant themselves on our subconscious even if we are not aware of what we are singing.

When you read the words to a song, do not assume that because you know it musically that you know it lyrically. I love the song by Aerosmith, "Last Child," because of its cool groove and musical spacing. When Nathan heard it, he too fell in love with the groove just as I did. I almost approved the song but thought I'd take one last glance at the words. Unfortunately, there is a slang phrase in the chorus that is sexual in nature and degrading to women. I would have skipped right by it because I like the music. Remember, the lyrics are the first thing you need to look at.

Third, we do not approve songs that contain sexual innuendo. My youngest daughter's favorite radio station is Radio Disney (radiodisney.com). The radio announcers are fun and relevant to the preteen age group. They host call-in contests, speak with kids around the United States, and play energetic music. At any given time, you can hear classic Disney tunes like "I've Got No Strings" and "I Just Can't Wait to Be King." Along with these, they also play today's teen pop songs like Hannah Montana's "Best of Both Worlds" and Jonas Brothers' "Hold On."

Occasionally, Radio Disney plays songs that are more mainstream. One such song is "Who Let the Dogs Out" by the Baha Men. At first blush, the song has a fun, Caribbean beat and talks about some disrespectful men who are troublemakers at a party. As I listened to the song, learning and singing the lyrics, it dawned on me that there was more to this than just disruptive partygoers. There is a very subtle innuendo of sexual activity. If you don't know the slang, then you may not catch it, but it's there. Without thinking, I was letting my children hear and form in their minds a picture that was far from appropriate for them.

Another song that is popular as of this writing is Soulja Boy's "Crank That." This one violates our guidelines in so many ways. Heavy cultural accents and slang disguise foul language and sexual innuendo through the music. The group even has a cute little dance that helps in taking the focus off the words.

Hear what I am saying, and what I am not saying. I am not condemning a style of music but I am rejecting inappropriate messages contained in the music. I am not saying that groups like The Baha Men or Soulja Boy are evil or Satan worshippers. (There are some, I know there are.) What I am saying, or rather warning, is that no matter what the source, you, as a parent, need to evaluate the lyrics of every song that potentially will live in your household.

Whenever Nathan and I run across a song that has lyrics that may or may not be appropriate, we ask ourselves, "Could I read these words out loud to my grandmother without being embarrassed?"

Once we see that the lyrics are permissible, we ask the second question . . .

Question 2
What picture does the song paint?

This is a deeper question than merely what the lyrics *say*. Language is more than stringing words together. Communication goes deeper that just the words. The message that a song delivers rides on the back of the words and explodes in the mind of the hearer.

> The message that a song delivers
> rides on the back of the words and
> explodes in the mind of the hearer.

Think of Leonardo da Vinci's masterpiece, *Mona Lisa*. More than likely, you can see her simple brown hair and gentle grin. Some say that she is the most recognizable woman in all of history and that she is the masterpiece of masterpieces. Why? Is it the type of paint that da Vinci used in his creation? Is it the pressure that he applied at different points in the painting that create depth? The effect of the specific colors he used? What is it that makes her a masterpiece? For most, it is not one aspect of the painting but the totality of it.

The picture a song paints is the same way. A guitar solo may resonate with you or you might like the repetition of a phrase, but the picture that the lyrics paint in your mind is a combination of it all. The question is, can you look at that picture and not have it cause you or your child to stumble? Can you show that picture to your spouse, to your friend, to your pastor?

Remember our discussion on sexual innuendo? Many songs played on the Top 40 charts paint inappropriate pictures of a desire for the opposite sex. In Flo Rida's song "Low," the artist describes a woman walking out on a club dance floor. While the other patrons are looking on, she begins to do a dance that imitates

Nathan's Note

Music isn't just entertainment. It has a lot of power that affects your lifestyle too. It shows who you are and who you want to be. Choose music wisely. Remember that emotions and mood go together. Believe me, I know.

sex. Even without an MTV video, most of us can picture the moves.

Another example is the song "Bubbly" by Colbie Caillat. The simple guitar and light walking rhythm are very pleasant. Listening to the song, you feel like you're strolling casually in the park holding the hand of the one you love. The picture the lyrics paint is that of a cute relationship between two people. To his credit, my son Nathan caught another picture that the song portrays: A guy and girl snuggling together in bed. Yes, you could argue that they may be married and they may just be keeping warm. For Nathan and me, the picture was a bit more intimate, and that kind of intimacy is too adult for children and teens.

Other songs paint mental images of extreme violence or destructive lifestyles. In Ice-T's song "Squeeze the Trigger," he describes a lifestyle of guns and gangs. He says that he is merely describing the world in which he grew up but is that the atmosphere that you desire for your children?

Question 3
What is the mood or feel of the song?

Does the song bring you up, bring you down, or neither? Could you picture this song being played during a scary movie, a Disney flick, or a love story? The *mood* of sound, like the ambience of lighting, affects our emotions. (Recall track 2, page 31.)

Music is mostly rhythmic. There are groups, genres, and songs out there that don't have any meter or time to them. They are free flowing. When listening to Imogen Heap's song "Hide and Seek," you feel like you're listening to someone speak rather than sing. However, most songs have a rhythm to them. That pulse, combined with the chording of the song, can create a mood in the listener faster than a high-speed download.

Song mood is important because it can affect the overall mood of the listener. Over time, that mood can sink into the soul and permeate the way a person thinks, acts, and feels. We have all heard the stories about serial killers listening to dark music before embarking on their rampage. Mood and feel are critical for a longer-term look at how the playlist of your child affects her overall attitude.

I want to be honest about a struggle that Nathan and I went through recently. For the longest time, Nathan wanted to download the song "Back in Black" by AC/DC. As a musician, he enjoyed the combination of the steady beat and

> **Nathan's Note**
> Buying the song "Back in Black" by AC/DC was something I really wanted to do. To me, the lead singer's raspy voice adds to the flavor of the song. My dad thought he was just yelling. I didn't think so.
>
> What we both agreed on was that the music was great, driving, pure Rock 'n' Roll. We battled back and forth on it. I kept reminding him that according to the guidelines, there was nothing wrong with the lyrics. For me, the mood was OK too. Finally, he gave in. He had to. The guidelines said the song passed. I know that ultimately, he has the say-so. But for now, it's on my playlist.

salty guitar solos. However, I just couldn't see it. Maybe it was because it brought me back to my youth. When I was in high school, the song "Back in Black" was always blasted through the speakers of a boom box (remember those?) by the head-banger, druggie group that sat on the curb after school and smoked cigarettes. I was not eager to say yes to my son's request.

After long discussions that lasted for several weeks, I could not deny that the song met the criteria. The lyrics do not portray any sexual innuendo or bad language, and the melodies were singable. I even researched the song's history and title and nothing stuck out as reprehensible.[2] The song drives hard but it is the mood that raised a red flag for me. The song seems angry. It seems bitter. It seems full of "attitude." Combine that with *my* past experience, and I wrestled with that one. Yet, I still could not deny that the guidelines that Nathan and I established permitted the song. Finally, I allowed Nathan to download the song and add it to his "Nathan Rawks" playlist (right next to songs by Relient K and Skillet). He knows, however, that if his mood changes negatively as a result of listening to this or any other song, I will delete it.

Mood is very important. As we said before, music can change our emotions as it syncs up with the internal rhythms of our souls. Many songs fit all the guidelines but are just plain dark. They bring you low, they make you angry, and they transport you into a trancelike state. I watch these very carefully. Let me rephrase that: I watch *Nathan* listen to these very carefully. If I sense his mood change negatively for, say, a week or two, his playlist (among other life aspects) is one of the first areas I screen.[3]

OK. So far we've said that the parent is the one who makes the final decisions in the house regarding music but not without input from the child. We've screened song lyrics and imagined the picture they create in our minds. We've focused on the mood of the song, and now we ask a question that incorporates the people around us.

Question 4
Will the song cause others to stumble?

We are a society that looks out for itself. As a friend of mine once said, "We are all tuned in to that radio station WIIFM: What's In It For Me?" Pervasive selfish attitudes are somewhat expected in the world, but they've permeated our relationships within the church as well. How often have congregational families split because of worship style, dunk or no-dunk baptism, or speaking in tongues? Out-of-balance individualism has even wreaked havoc on many churches today. Jesus-followers who, by definition, are part of God's family, turn on each other and refuse to talk through issues and differences. They destroy relationships rather than lovingly defer to a brother or sister in Christ.

This is not that different from the church in the first century. The apostle Paul was constantly dealing with the effects of unhealthy individualism among Christians. Infidelity, corrupt clergy, and lawsuits among the brethren all plagued the early church.

Paul combats this hyper-individualism by using a situation common to his day. There were certain foods the new Jesus-followers ate that were not harmful to them spiritually. However, they were still surrounded by many people burdened with an old religious structure that said it was a sin to eat these foods. Rather than encouraging them to just "do their own thing"—instead of dismissing others' "hangups"—Paul instructed the Christians to exercise restraint for the sake of others' faith.

> Let us therefore make every effort to do what leads to peace and to mutual edification. Do not destroy the

work of God for the sake of food. All food is clean, but it is wrong for a man to eat anything that causes someone else to stumble. It is better not to eat meat or drink wine or to do anything else that will cause your brother to fall. (Romans 14:19–21)

Paul was aware that one of the key elements to healthy Christian relationships was not causing another person to stumble in faith because of your own actions. He was resolute in teaching Christians to watch out for others and not to be so wrapped up in themselves.[4]

Bring all that to our music choices. Would the music to which we listen cause another person to question his faith or be overly offended by the words or style? Is a hard rock song appropriate to blast in a room filled with two-year-olds? These are the types of questions that I monitor as a dad. Nathan does a pretty good job of reading who is in the room when he's listening to music but I am hypersensitive about it, primarily because the New Testament is also.

Final question . . .

Question 5
Who is the artist or group?

Moms and Dads, this question forces you to make some tough decisions. In today's student culture, the bands that write the songs are pop idols. Students follow the inside lives of band members and groups, wishing their lives were like that. How many teenage girls have wanted to be Hannah Montana—a TV star and pop singer all in one! (I have one of these lemming children in my household as we speak.) As a parent, I am always encouraged when one of these diva pop stars makes a statement about the purity of her life and the goal of holding true to morality. Albeit skeptical, my opinion of these singers and bands is positive. I have found that in every generation, there is a cadre of bands and musicians like these that continue to restore hope to the music world.

. . . .

They claim to know God, but by their actions they deny him. They are detestable, disobedient and unfit for doing anything good.
–Titus 1:16

. . . .

On the flip side of the album, there are bands that churn out great songs that meet the rest of the criteria, but the band or artist may be a flat-out devil worshipper! Their lifestyle, look, and comments emulate only things of the Devil. They completely live for themselves and have shut off any acknowledgment of something greater than the next fix, paycheck, or ego trip.

Even more dangerous bands are the ones that are subtle in their lyrics and music. They write songs and live lives that seem holy and draw large followings. God talks about this type of people when He says, "They claim to know God, but by their actions they deny him. They are detestable, disobedient and unfit for doing anything good" (Titus 1:16).

For Nathan and me, certain bands and artists are simply off limits. Marilyn Manson is a no. Eminem is a no. Soulja Boy is a no. We came to that conclusion based on the history of their foul language, explicit sexual references, and God-hating

Nathan's Note

Obviously, being thirteen, I want more freedom for everything. I also want the best for myself and I know that my dad can make the best decision for me at the moment. As I get older, I know there will be more freedom to choose music for myself. I also know that means more responsibility. These guidelines are great training for my future decisions!

songs. For us, they are off our list.

There are other bands out there that are called crossover bands. These are artists whose songs can be heard on "Christian" and "Secular" music stations alike. Artists like Skillet, Flyleaf, or The Fray are popular with all teenagers. If you study these bands, overall, the songs they write are either loving life songs or loving other people songs. Their lifestyle is clean (for lack of a better word). In other words, you won't read about them in the daily tabloids; at least not as of this publication.

There you have it. These are the basic questions that form the filter through which Nathan and I sift all of our music choices. They may be ones you adopt; they may not. The key reason for these questions is to foster a godly conversation about what is happening in your music world. And you and your child need to have those types of godly conversations.

The Positive Results

As of this writing, Nathan and I have been at this for a few years. Weekly, he presents me with song lyrics and we work the guidelines together. We talk about the songs, why the other kids at school like them, and if they are appropriate for him. The results of this process have been greater than just the yes-or-no music decision. We have found five benefits from having these guidelines:

Benefit 1: As a parent, I am also held accountable by the guidelines. As a 1980s Rock 'n' Roller, I have always enjoyed the harder, driving rock style. However, the songs that Nathan brings to me have awakened my musical taste buds for the new sounds of today. I have been exposed to a world of music that I never would have glanced at if it were not for his passion for different types of music. On the flip side, I have deleted songs from my MP3 player—songs that I used to love (and maybe still do) but that do not fit our guidelines. For example, "Every Rose Has Its Thorn" by Poison was a recent deletion on my part due to sexual innuendo.

Benefit 2: My child is empowered to make choices. Nathan, too, has discovered a new world of music. Because he knows that the guidelines are there to protect him, he has a sense of freedom when listening to music. He knows the boundaries and tries to keep within them. He feels valued and empowered because I allow him to make choices within the context of the guidelines.

Foster Kline and Charles Fay wrote a great parenting book called *Parenting with Love and Logic.*[5] The whole premise of the book is to allow your child to make choices that are appropriate for them and agreeable for you as the parent. The key is allowing the choice to be made within the context of acceptable guidelines. For example, a mom lays out two sets of clothing and allows her child to choose between them. The child takes ownership of the decision and her confidence increases. These results are the same with music guidelines. Confidence, encouragement, and ownership in Nathan; peace of mind for me!

Benefit 3: There is a reduction of risk. Nathan is a great kid! We have not had major rebellion issues or arguments in our relationship. I am not so naïve as to think there will not be any. In fact, as a thirteen-year-old, he tests the boundaries of his freedoms quite often.

Truthfully, he probably has a song or two we would consider grey in the color scheme of acceptance. However, the guidelines reduce the risk of Nathan intentionally or unintentionally falling in love with a song that is downright bad. As we discussed earlier, songs have a way of grabbing hold of us and changing our attitudes and behavior. The guidelines act as filters that allow the good and keep out the bad.

Benefit 4: We are free to listen to the songs on our playlist—guilt free! One of the radio stations here that plays "Christian" music had a great commercial on the air. It is simply people giving a one-sentence statement on the benefits of listening to that particular station. One mom, her voice shaking with gratitude and emotion says, "I can allow my kids to listen to the radio and not worry about what's going into their minds." What parent could argue with that one!

These guidelines have freed my mind of parental guilt, because I know what Nathan has on his MP3 player. They have given Nathan the freedom to listen to and enjoy approved songs without the fear of being in trouble with Dad. They have allowed us to talk freely about songs and music without our discussion ending up in an argument, as I know happens with many families. They have set both of us free to listen to our playlists without the fear (or embarrassment) of inappropriate songs.

Benefit 5 (and most important): We enjoy an ongoing conver-

sation and relationship. My dad is an incredible musician. All my life, I remember listening to my mom and him play the multiple instruments hanging around our house and enjoying every minute of it. As a choral director, he would often compose music for various occasions and use our family to test out his harmonies. I remember the first time he asked my opinion of how the tenor part "felt" and "flowed." To this day, I cannot recall the song, but I do know I did not like it—the tenor part anyway—and I let him know. After a brief dialogue, he changed the tenor line based on our give-and-take.

Inside, I was elated. Not because he took my advice, not because the song turned out better (which it did, thank you very much), but because my dad and I talked it through and he listened to my advice. Together we made something better. Not his song, but our relationship.

The greatest benefit of these guidelines is the discussion that Nathan and I have together and the relationship building that follows. We have had some great times imitating Neil Pert's drum solo in "Tom Sawyer" and Van Halen's keyboard riff in "Jump." We've analyzed old Michael W. Smith songs and contrasted them with songs by Relient K and Big Daddy Weave. We've taken turns air-guitaring Queen solos and singing the songs by Brooke Fraser.

Remember that over and above simply choosing music, the primary purpose of this book is to foster conversations between you—the parent—and your child. The guidelines are suggested. You may change them if you like. However, we have found that opening up a loving dialogue and the closer relationship we share as a result is even more important than the guidelines that result from the conversation.

Nathan and I have seen positive results from these guidelines. He feels empowered to make his own music decisions and I feel confident in exercising my parental authority based on the guidelines. Together, we are constantly in conversation that, as a by-product, has strengthened our relationship. God is honored; our relationship is strengthened. What can be better than that?

Chapter Exercise

Step 1: Ask your child to give you the lyrics to one or two favorite songs.

Step 2: Read the lyrics together out loud, taking note of your child's reaction and your own reaction.

Step 3: Listen to the song(s) together.

Step 4: Using the guidelines, rate the song(s) per question on a scale of 1 to 5 (1 being bad; 5 being good).

1. What do the lyrics say?

2. What picture does this song paint?

3. What is the mood or feel of the song?

4. Will the song cause others to stumble?

5. Who is the artist or the group?

Step 5: Discuss the appropriateness of the song(s) based on the score. If the song rates 20–25, it's a safe bet that it's OK for your child. 15–20, some deeper discussion needs to happen. 14 and below, better dump it. Remember that you have the ultimate say-so because YOU are the parent.

Recap

✔ Remember that the purpose of this book is to initiate conversation between you and your child regarding the music to which they want to listen. There are guidelines that Nathan and I use that suit us. They may not all work for you and your child. That's your call.

✔ The Guidelines: Filtering a song through a set of questions helps to sort out good from not-so-good music choices. The overarching rule is that you as the parent make the final decision (even if your child doesn't like it).

✔ Question 1: What do the lyrics say? For us, if the lyrics denounce God, take His name in vain, have cuss words or obvious sexual innuendo, the song is out.

✔ Question 2: What picture does the song paint? Communication is more than words. It paints a picture. When you hear a song, what picture pops into your mind?

✔ Question 3: What is the mood or feel of the song? Does the song bring you up or bring you down or neither?

Variety in mood is OK but if your child is listening to songs that are consistently dark, you may want to address it.

✔ Question 4: Will the song cause others to stumble? A song may be fine for you and your child, but if the child were to play it in public, would others be offended? If yes, then you have to decide whether to keep the song and be discrete, or chuck it.

✔ Question 5: Who is the artist or the group? For us, there are a few bands to which we just say no. Most are neutral.

✔ We have found five benefits to these guidelines:

1. As a parent, I am also held accountable by the guidelines.

2. My child is empowered to make choices.

3. There is a reduction of risk.

4. We are free to listen to the songs on our playlist—guilt-free!

5. Most importantly, we enjoy an ongoing conversation and relationship.

track 5

"Let's Be Honest"

The Legal Issues

He who has been stealing must steal no longer.
—EPHESIANS 4:28

Integrity is telling myself the truth. And honesty is telling the truth to other people.
—SPENCER JOHNSON

In the early 1960s, compact audio cassettes began to be mass-produced for public distribution in Europe. Their popularity quickly spread and the rush for product expansion went into high gear. The Mercury Record Company, a U.S. affiliate of Philips, brought these audio cassettes to the United States in September of 1966 and the age of "music on hand" was born.[1]

Since those initial offerings of personal music accessibility, the recording industry has gone through unprecedented technological advancement. In 1990, the first CD player/recorder hit the market. The Philips Company had developed a machine that would not only play the plastic, laser-encoded disc but had the ability to record onto it as well. The electronics industry scrambled to produce these CD player/recorders in mass numbers as the demand for the compact discs grew astronomically. People paid hefty prices to be able to record music onto a CD for playback but as the price for these players continued to drop, more and more people discovered the convenience of recording studio quality music for personal use.

However, this convenience led to another music recording industry that grew as quickly as the original source, and that was the music piracy industry. Street corner vendors sell knockoff CDs at a fraction of the price with just as much clarity and quality as the original. Those who monitored copyright violations could not keep up with the onslaught of infringements as peer-to-peer networks effortlessly traded songs worldwide. Kids with friends, adults with coworkers, churches with church-workers, the list of infringements is endless and, in most cases, unintentional.

....

> While it may seem innocent and a
> minor violation, music piracy is still
> just that . . . *piracy.*

....

Call it copyright infringement or rights violation, acquiring songs outside of the legal bounds is piracy. According to Dictionary.com, a pirate is "a person who uses or reproduces the work or invention of another without authorization."[2]

With the ease of music access that the Internet provides and the technology of duplication that is readily available to almost anyone, music piracy has become big business. According to the International Federation of the Phonographic Industry, one in three music discs sold worldwide is an illegal copy, creating a $4.6 billion music bootleg market.[3]

Many parents and children do not realize the legal issues and boundaries that exist in the music world. They believe that once music is in their hands they are free to do with it what they will, not understanding the legal nor spiritual violations they create.[4]

While it may seem innocent and a minor violation, music piracy is still just that . . . *piracy.* Violating these legal curbs is against God's will for the Christ-follower. Among other Scripture verses, God reminds us in 1 Peter 2 that those who call themselves Christian should especially be sensitive to the authorities and the laws they have established.[5]

Submit yourselves for the Lord's sake to every authority instituted among men: whether to the king, as the supreme authority, or to governors, who are sent by him to punish those who do wrong and to commend those who do right. For it is God's will that by doing good you should silence the ignorant talk of foolish men. (1 Peter 2:13–15)

Frankly, the legal issues are not all that confusing.[6] Most are pretty clear even though most are neglected. Basically, authors own the exclusive rights to what they produce. They have the say-so on how their work is to be replicated. This is called a *copyright* and it protects the author of the music from being ripped off.

In general, the copyright law says that if any music or lyrics are under protection of the copyright law, it is illegal to:

+ Reproduce music or lyrics without permission,

+ Distribute the music or lyrics either for free, for no profit, or for profit,

+ Perform the music or lyrics as a performance in a public setting,

+ Play the recorded music or lyrics in public, even if you own the CD,

+ Imitate the song or make an arrangement of the song for a performance in a public setting. (Yes, I believe that Weird Al Yankovich has copyrights for his parodies.)

Most churches and organizations purchase a yearly license to play and reproduce their music. Most individuals do not.

However, this doesn't mean you need to purchase a license to download music. The legitimate music stores (like iTunes and AmazonMP3) license the public use of the song when you buy it.

The time when most children get into trouble is when they file-share over the Internet. This means they put a song on YouTube or e-mail it to a friend. That is illegal because they are making copies of the song and distributing it for free.

There are a plethora of situations that you'll run into with your child. Even now, I'm thinking about all the times I've illegally given my worship team, friends, and relatives music that was protected by copyright. (*Father, forgive me.*)

If you have more questions about this area, type in "copyright infringement" in your search engine or go to the government's Web site at http://www.copyright.gov.

Recap

✔ The United States Copyright Law protects all produced music. Most people don't know or don't care about that when it comes to reproducing or sharing music.

✔ Because God calls us to obey the authorities, you need to take the lead with your child to make sure the law is not broken.

✔ The general rule is that no music can be reproduced, altered, or played publicly without the proper copyright permission.

notes

· ·

track 1

1. Dean Goodman, "Smokey Robinson Bares His Soul in Gospel Foray," *Yahoo News*, April 28, 2004, http://story.news .yahoo.com/news?tmpl=story&cid=638&ncid=762&e= 1&u=/nm/20040428/en_nm/leisure_robinson_dc (accessed January 2, 2008).

2. See Numbers 18:12, 29.

3. Quotation found in various online sources, and in *An Encyclopedia of Quotations About Music*, ed. Nat Shapiro (New York: Doubleday, 1978).

4. Louie Giglio, quoted by David Orland in "When Music Is Our Enemy," Boundless.org webzine, August 2, 2001, http:// www.boundless.org/2005/articles/a0000459.cfm (accessed June 5, 2008).

track 2

1. *The Shawshank Redemption*, directed by Frank Darabont (Castle Rock, 1994); based on the short novel, *The Shawshank Redemption* by Stephen King.

2. Dictionary.com Unabridged (v 1.1), *The American Heritage Dictionary of the English Language*, 4th ed., s.v. "power," http:// dictionary.reference.com/browse/power (accessed October 10, 2007).

3. Steven C. Martin, Rebecca L. Collins, Marc N. Elliott, et al., "Exposure to Degrading Versus Nondegrading Music Lyrics

and Sexual Behavior Among Youth," *Pediatrics* 118, no. 2 (August 2006): e430–e441, http://pediatrics.aappublications .org/cgi/content/full/118/2/e430.

4. Ibid.

5. Natasha Ramsey quoted by Sunil Vyas, "Raunchy Lyrics Trigger Earlier Onset of Sexual Activity Among Teens: Study," *EarthTimes*, August 7, 2006, http://www.earthtimes .org/articles/show/7987.html (accessed January 5, 2009).

6. Basil Nortz, "The Moral Power of Music," Catholic Education Resource Center, http://www.catholiceducation.org/articles/ arts/al0221.html (accessed November 15, 2008); first published in *The Homiletic & Pastoral Review* (April 2002): 17–22.

7. BrainyQuotes.com Quotations. "Lenny Kravitz Quotes," Brainymedia.com, retrieved January 22, 2009, http://www .brainyquote.com/quotes/quotes/l/lennykravi333776.html.

8. Mary A. VanDerWeele, "Staying in Tune with Music," BNET, http://findarticles.com/p/articles/mi_m0826/is_n4_v8/ ai_12426666/ (accessed September 17, 2008); from *Vibrant Life* (July–August 1992).

9. Julius Portnoy quoted by David Tame, *The Secret Power of Music* (Rochester, VT: Destiny Books, 1984), 138.

10. Incrediblehorizons.com, "Psychoacoustics," http://www .incrediblehorizons.com/psychoacoustics.html (accessed August 18, 2009).

track 3

1. Dictionary.com Unabridged (v 1.1), *The American Heritage Dictionary of the English Language*, 4th ed., s.v., "genre," http:// dictionary.reference.com/browse/genre (accessed November 12, 2007).

2. For a deeper discussion, see Kimberly Smith, *Music and Morals* (Enumclaw, WA: Winepress, 2005).

track 4

1. One online resource is The Source for Youth Ministry at http://www.thesource4ym.com/teenlingo/. Another is Focus on the Family at http://www.family.org/.
2. If you'd like a brief history of songs, a good Web site is http://www.songfacts.com.
3. CAUTION: If your child displays excessive low moods for a long period of time, don't be naïve. Their music choice is not the only thing going on. Talk to them calmly and honestly. Get help from a professional if necessary.
4. See Philippians 2:4.
5. Updated edition (Colorado Springs, CO: Pinon Press, June 5, 2006).

track 5

1. For the history of sound recording and production, see David L. Morton Jr., *Sound Recording: The Life Story of a Technology* (Westport, CT: Greenwood, 2004).
2. Dictionary.com Unabridged (v 1.1), *The American Heritage Dictionary of the English Language*, 4th ed., s.v., "pirate," http://dictionary.reference.com/browse/pirate (accessed January 21, 2008).
3. IFPI (International Federation of the Phonographic Industry) press release (London, Madrid), "One in Three Music Discs Is Illegal but Fight Back Starts to Show Results," June 23, 2005, http://www.ifpi.org/content/section_news/20050623.html (accessed August 2, 2008).

4. For more statistics, go to the online article, "Fewer Than 1 in 10 Teenagers Believe That Music Piracy Is Morally Wrong," http://barna.org/barna-update/article/5-barna-update/ 139-fewer-than-1-in-10-teenagers-believe-that-music-piracy -is-morally-wrong.

5. See also Romans 13:1–3 and Titus 3:1–2.

6. Obviously, the Copyright Law is long and detailed. The basics as it applies to this publication are taken from the online government resource found at http://www.copyright.gov/.

about the authors

Todd Stocker is a pastor, church planter, communicator, and writer. His devotionals and articles have been published in *Living Magazine, The Lutheran Witness,* and *Connect Quarterly.* A nationally sought-after communicator and winner of the Rickman Award for Creative Communication, Stocker has been the keynote speaker at youth camps, men's and women's ministry events, and chamber of commerce luncheons.

Nathan Stocker, a freshman at the Saint Paul Conservatory for Performing Artists in St. Paul, MN, is studying contemporary music through guitar expressions. He helped his dad organize and lead his middle school chapel band, and likes to play and compose music and hang out with friends in his spare time. Nathan has been student body president and a member of National Junior Honor Society.